if

KIMBERLEY JONATHAN BEARD

If
Copyright © 2021 by Kimberley Jonathan Beard

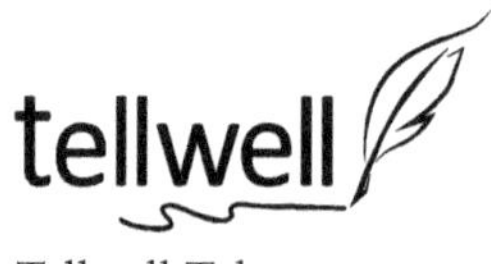

Tellwell Talent
www.tellwell.ca

ISBN
978-0-2288-5467-8 (Paperback)
978-0-2288-5466-1 (eBook)

TO

Beryl, Barbara, Sarah, and Mugsie

and

all who dare to ask, **If...**

Table of Contents

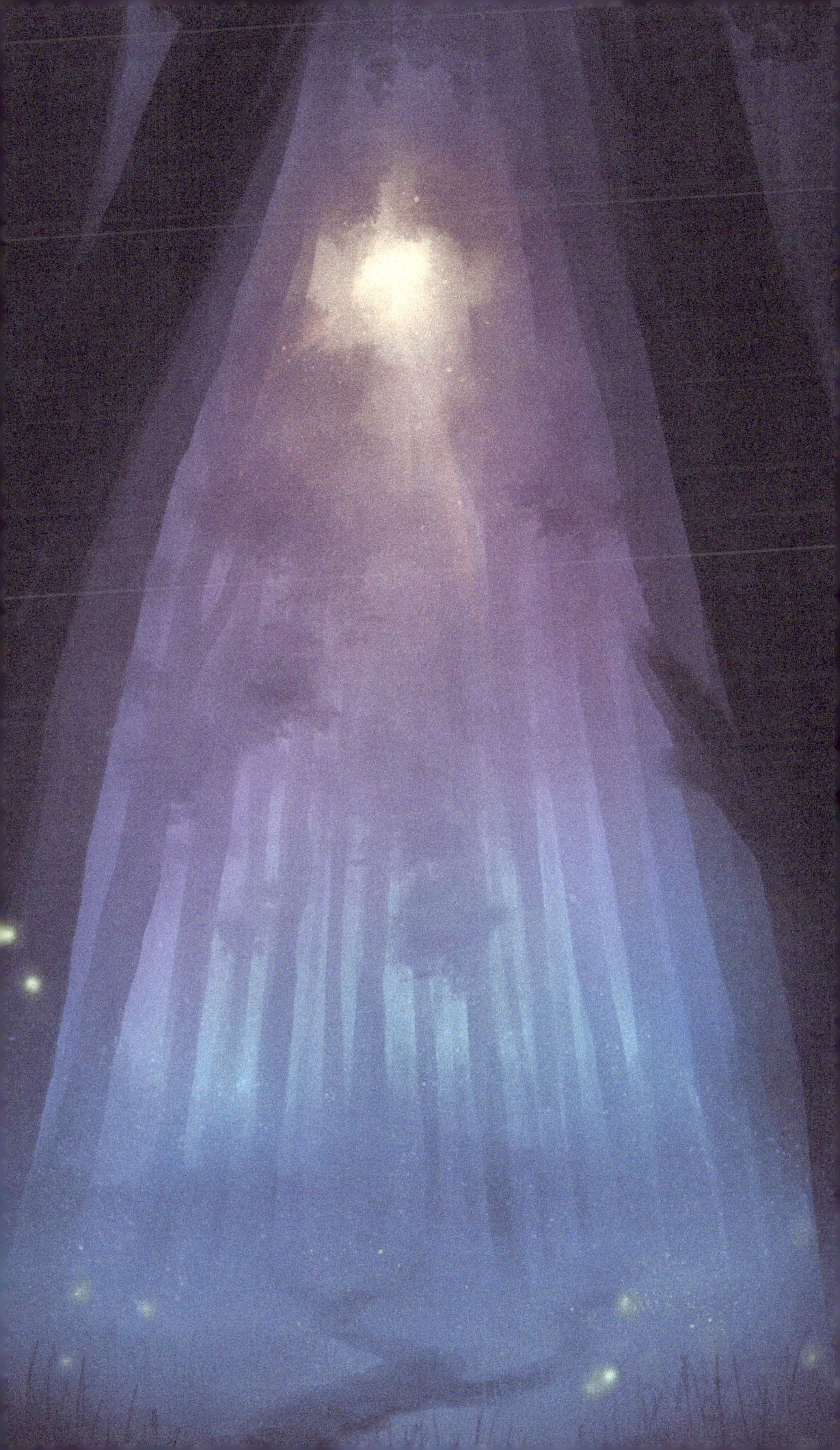

Names on a Wall

Light pokes through bullet holes
     pin pricks, painful and revealing
a fearful relic scarring holy doors

Family pictures, bloodstained rags, scattered bones
     all that remains, to tell the story of what happened
who is to blame

Names on a wall, the murdered, disappeared ones
     cry out for justice, in this silent hall
But it is telling, that there will be no meaningful reply
     only empty excuses that echo
I was following orders
I didn't know
I didn't want to know
I am not to blame

Why is this grotesque scene repeated again and again
     Cambodia, Rwanda, El Salvador, Ethiopia, Spain?
It is this! Our bloody human condition
     a shared fault of ruinous pain
that we can so easily destroy others, because they are others
     leaving only *we*, the diminished…
          to remain.

The Choosing

The trail is rocky, overgrown…
               forgotten
No footprint nor luxuriant moss
               is broken
Taking the path less travelled
            in silence—I am beholden.

Would this turn or that
            have made a difference?
would a word softly spoken
            have moved your heart…

Changed my mind to choose
            what I could not see?
a choice, with breath, long held…
               lamented

This is the path I choose
            and in the choosing
found that love is sometimes
              gained…
                  in losing

Drowning Slowly

My face slides
        below
                the shimmering surface

I don't want to stop-
            cool, enveloping, revealing
                  submerged things

Looking down, not up, seeing what lies
            beneath

So, let me drown in your love
            sinking slowly
                slipping silently

joined forever…
            never wanting to return

Touching Hearts

I thought of you and smiled
hands touching
                        fingers dancing
                                    to the rhythms of love

eyes burning
                          longing
                              hoping

asking if you, only you would…

touch me
            speak what is unspoken

grasp my hands
                embrace my desire

draw it close to your heart

                      and say…love.

Drifting

When a heart is broken
    what words can be spoken…

Like a wave upon the shore
    your love overwhelms me
and then…
            withdraws

Leaving me gasping
    and crying out…

                more

Crashing foam, incandescent light
    drawing me in…
                casting me out

Twirling, swirling, tossed to and fro
    I wait, heart in hand
for the next wave…
                to kiss the sand

When a heart is broken
    what words can be spoken…

Runes

Let me tell you a saga…
a tale of dreams, visions, songs
words softly spoken

Eyes fixed, following
as embers crackle and fly…
          up, up, to the night sky

To Valhalla's halls, where dreams–
the things we treasure most…
          never die

Ears burning
whispered words of love…
          gently spoken

To touch your breast
feel the rhythm of your heart
and wonder, breathlessly…
          at your visage here

I would tell you of my love
of dreams become real
and of delight found…
          in you.

I Should Know

What are you longing for?
laughter, a space to become…

> a warm embrace

A song to sing, a tale to tell
a listening heart, to hear words unspoken
or a tear that cries out… *yes*

What are you longing for?
the reflection of love in my eyes
soft words to enfold and caress you…

> then gather you in

To be precious, wanted, an object of desire
a wave searching for a shore
a planet for a star

What are you longing for?

The Burning

The fire dances upwards before my eyes
   its heat and shimmering flames leap high
as if to call out…

            and invite me to draw nigh

Listen to the rhythm of my entrancing light
   and find in its warmth
the answer to the question you have come to ask…

                but could not speak

Why does your heart not burn with passion
   like the embers in my fire?
where is your fervor, your hope…

            your desire

So, learn from me
   burn wild, consumed by love and life
and find in the offering…

          your own fulfilling.

Let Sleeping Dogs Lie

do not disturb
    their dreaming…
underneath

the rustling palm tree
    brown dogs, black dogs
and me, all seeking shade
    respite from the midday sun

What do you dream of?
    sand flying
from your nostrils

Do you dream of a world
    where no stones are thrown
where none go hungry
    a home where you are wanted?

We are Morpheus's companions
    strange menagerie softly breathing
together dreaming, and we agree
    to let sleeping dogs lie.

IF...

I dreamed of a world so pure
in which only love endures

where church bells ring to say
I love you more
with each passing day

if dreams could only be...

Night Sky

I watched as those silent, shimmering orbs
>slipped from the sky
>>and descended to the sea

Where they became
>glittering diamonds beyond counting
>>save the two
>>>that found their home....
>>>>in you.

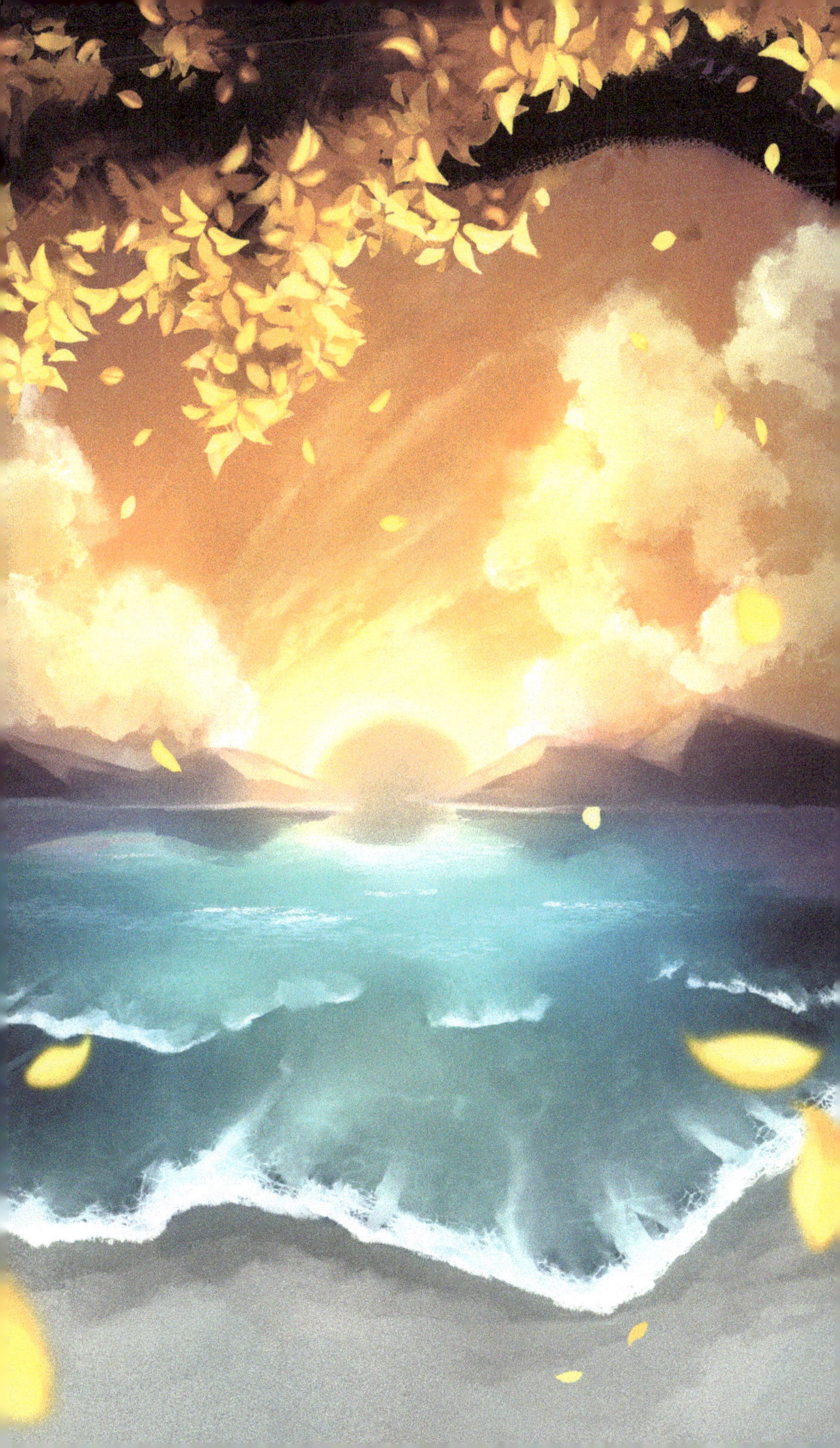

loon calls to silence

misty dawn canoe dancer

water dream catcher

incandescent blue

white cloud boats drifting westward

red sun chases night

white snow flake dancing

swirling wind tear caressed

sky to silence falls

rain drops dance with wind

then abandon her embrace

heaven falls to earth

Mud Between My Toes

squish, squash
caressing my soul
squish, squash

Deep sliding impression
squish, squash
red ochre of life
squish, squash

Pressed deep, moist, embracing
squish, squash
gentle rain, pools that tremble
squish, squash

My essence, my journey's end
squish, squash
mud between my toes.

Waiting for the Rains to Come

Thirsty soil, crocodile tree
   thorn bush, ochre angel dust
sun and blood red sky…
               all waiting for the rains to come

Ex-presidents, beggars in the street
   school children with running feet
lovers, arms entwined, meander…
               all waiting for the rains to come

Sentinels of the night, shimmering eyes
   a policeman drooping at the gate
crowing rooster, barking dog…
               all waiting for the rains to come

My heart in lonely silence waits
   an empty field, hungry for the farmer's plow
a village hut with roof bowed low…
               all waiting for the rains to come.

Joy in the Morning

Children's laugher echoes, translucent
walls of cardboard, plastic and tin
morning mist mingles… rising smoke…
cooking fires aglow

Dogs bark, bicycle tires squelch in blood red mud
feet fall, syncopated rhythms
as the rising golden orb…
drives off shades of night

Yellow juicy mangos lie sleepily on wooden tables
beside chapati, roasted maize and mandazi golden
all waiting for customers to pay the shilling…
then call out *asante sana* and *mzuri sana*

Kibera awakes, feet stomping
an urban rhythmic drum
vibrant songs of hope…
without hunger, fear, or ancient ghosts

The ancestors too
come to watch, ponder
then dance with joy…
at this new day's wonder.

Irie

Island of coral, Jah's gift
    kissed by the sun's fiery touch
skyward jump up
    bury me whole in this place

Earth, water, wind, fire
    rum, cool ocean breeze
the breath of life
    sage Cotton trees bend to listen as…

Ancient drums beat new rhythms
    freedom, hope, becoming
a new world of promise, or is it…
    duppies whispering… *Irie.*

Temples

A man with empty box came walking
    eyes glazed, hands waving, voice crying
My treasures are gone… only emptiness remains

And I, sat silent
    an unwelcome witness
to a conversation with no reply

Madness, rum or loneliness
    it filled his empty box until the cardboard, brown and worn
burst forth with tears
    holey evocation and words that cloy

And what of my box, my sacred temple?
    what treasures, burdens, regrets and joys
do I clutch while striving to dissemble

A man with empty box came walking
    eyes glazed, hands waving, voice crying
My treasures are gone… only emptiness remains.

Nutmeg and Spices

The full moon casts a duppies light
    running feet, distant tunnel voices echo in the dark
a goat in the bush, a dog in the street
    a dollar and a half to drop me at St. George's dragon's feet

Warm gentle breeze, blaring horn
    Mitsubishi rhythms drift past, calling out… *stop here*
rum shop figures lyme, cigarettes glowing
    laughter, loud voices and dominos

                        dizzily

                            descending

Sweet smelling spices, nutmeg lingers
    embraces me… seduces me… drawing me in
I laugh and shyly smile, for here I've found
    a foretaste of heaven, within these earthly bounds.

Night Rhythms

Trumpets… blare
    a guitarron beat… tremors
bodies weave patterns in Garibaldi time
    on this a Mariachi Sunday night

Accordion, harp, violin and vihuela
    rivals calling in the night
cigars, flowers, headlights passing by
    on this a Mariachi Sunday night

A song accepted… a song refused
    street children with hungry eyes call out
veinte Peso for a taco and a place to sleep
    on this a Mariachi Sunday night

The sad…the lonely… lovers hand in hand
    seek the rhythms of the heart
love songs that bring a tear… a smile
    on this a Mariachi Sunday night

And I…I sit … a silent witness
    to love…joy… and regret
just another pilgrim passing time
    on this a Mariachi Sunday night.

No Teeth in my Head

no shoes on my feet
    can you hear… what I cannot speak?

Listen… if you can
    to words unspoken
things left unsaid…

Put your hand here!
    feel my heart …tremble … beat
beating to the rhythms of memories gone
    and long-ago dreams… abandoned

We are not so different, you and me
    we both breathe… we both weep
in the end, shall we not join…
    in that final sleep

No teeth in my head
    no shoes on my feet
can you hear… what I cannot speak?

The Rickshaw Driver

Delhi night, diesel fumes and sweat
  bodies passing in and out of sight
round and round with a whispering sound
  saying pain and tears, ten rupees to eat…

       and then I sleep

Djinn chariot in dreamtime
  passing avatars asleep on cardboard cushions
a child cradled in her father's tender embrace
  a princess adorned with the jewels of love

An old man falling victim to his years
  eyes upturned to the stars
his mouth agape as if calling out to heaven
  but finding no words to speak…
dahl and rice, embers glowing, voices floating

All gone, left behind
  as the wheel of life revolves again…
leaving only…
   Delhi night, diesel fumes and sweat.

Café Dancing

Cigarettes, cell phones
women talking, walking
words float lightly…
                an evening breeze

Dog barking, cars passing
a flamenco of light and sound
a calle cacophony…
                alive with patas

People dance to rhythms only they can hear
going somewhere, nowhere
a camino…
                in colourful circles

And here I am, longing to dance
wanting what words cannot express
in Madrid…
                on a Saturday night.

Saint Mark's Bones

You have travelled far from
    Alexandria's distant shore
hidden by Venetian traders sure
    that your bones in barrel laid
were a treasure holy sufficient
    to redeem their trade.

A simple man of flesh and blood
    touched by divine love
drawn by the Master's call…
    follow me and surrender all

Follow you did, beset by love
    to find that in dying… in the giving
is life eternal…
    crowned by forgiving

And so, your bones await the Master's final call
    in this Byzantine reliquary resplendent
until dust, bone and ancient pall…
    are gathered into love.

Bridge of Sighs

Lover's embrace
    arms entwined
fingers tracing… lips caressing
    breath of life… love… sighs

A lone voyager watches
    cast upon San Marcos wooden shores
where sparkling glassy beads
    and humanities sea … drifts by

Picture boxes, moments stilled
    laughter, smiles, excited patter pass
leaving behind the T-shirts, trinkets
    almost Armanni … and masks

Still, a few ears are listening
    attuned to the long-ago voices in this place
which whisper of regret… *why… if only*

I can linger, but a moment
    before being tossed, twirled
caught in the flowing tides
    and leaving behind… only my sigh.

Gate of Heaven

Underground man
        marooned on an island of old clothes and tears
lies ignored… almost forgotten

Pooling pungent urine and sweat
        a slippery river of pain and despair
staring not at faces, but at shoes and feet
        that rise and fall… rise and fall

Then, four feet slow… and stop
        Get up the voices command
You, cannot die here!

Faint voices reply, as if from heaven
        echoing off these dark ceramic walls
There are other places to die
        whisper the ones who bled…
just up the stairs

But only the underground man can hear
        these ghostly visage voices
for this has become a spirit house
        for those without names, who die…
as the world walks by.

Avatars

Prayer wheels shimmer and spin
    incense smoke of burning bundles rise
pilgrims pass, some chanting on their knees
    offering prayers, seeking mercy and reprieve

Potala's winding pathway leads me upwards
    upwards to the sky palace
where cacophonous crowds converge
    and a still small voice dares whisper…

        one voice is missing

No Lama's chant in this place
    one face forbidden… one name unspoken
but written in the pilgrim's hearts
    a secret longing refuses to stay hidden

Flickering butter candles dim… but are not extinguished
    faces darkened by time flow past
an ancient wall worn smooth by faithful hands
    to where the scarring, new 'museum' portents stand

a crimson, red reminder that …

        one voice is missing.

Wind Songs

I was blown here from distant shores
    across an opaque ocean
scorched stone and shimmering sand
    a transient Harmattan mantle that rises and falls…
revealing, concealing

Over barrel markers
    Touareg nomads in night-coloured tents
ships of the desert at harbour…
    beside deep wells of life-giving water

Sandcastle forts
    crumbling walls... submerged
desert dunes that lean
    and then consume

They are reminders that this vast
    seemly empty quarter…
is a living contradiction
    of creation's wonder

Framed with still silence
    whispering wind song
all gathered here beneath…
    the resplendent sun.

Fearlessly Loving

The screen tells a story
    it's hard to believe
if you watch closely
    it's fear you perceive

Division, walls, shots in the dark
    another life gone but no one will speak
all that remains is a sadness
    a longing for justice and peace

Where is the hope, I am yearning to see?
    where is love, to dispel the darkness hiding in me
I want love…not fear
    to change direction and truly be

Who is my neighbour … why should I care?
    cries out my inner cynic with chronic despair
But you say… release your heart, do not be deceived
    for life, is found in loving… the very least of these

God grant me eyes wide open, to rise up and see
    that to love one another… is to believe
choose life over death, cast aside hate
    redeem fear with mercy, forgiveness and grace.

The Way

I have come to seek the way
having lost my bearings on other roads
a way which none can walk
unless called by name, to come…

Come join with others who also journey
the poor… the broken… those forgotten
all are welcome at His table
invited as they are…. prodigals found
those who seek a way back home

The way is found
not at my destination bound
but in silent soul moments
fused with pilgrims' laughter
reflection on the things that truly matter

It is a road, not well trodden
a way, long and winding
that calls me die to self
and find, in that unbinding
the God who whispers… love.

About the Author

Kimberley Jonathan Beard was born in Toronto, Canada. An adventurer at heart, he has hitchhiked across the Sahara Desert, taught in Nigeria and walked the Camino in Spain. He finds joy in learning from others and in seeking to be a 'citizen of the world' and a resident in the 'City of God'.

www.ingramcontent.com/pod-product-compliance
Lightning Source LLC
Chambersburg PA
CBHW050046040726
47599CB00015B/1830